PERSPECTIVE

God bless you
for supporting
hospice.

Bob Jacob

ALSO BY BOB JACOB

The Day Seamus Heaney Kissed My Cheek in Dublin

Upon Their Quiet Altars

PERSPECTIVE

Hospice Poems

by

Bob Jacob

Antrim House

Simsbury, Connecticut

Library of Congress Cataloging-in-Publication Data

Jacob, Bob, 1932-
Perspective : hospice poems / by Bob Jacob. -- 1st ed.
p. cm.
ISBN 978-0-9792226-6-5 (alk. paper)
1. Hospice care--Poetry. 2. Terminally ill--Poetry. I. Title.
PS3560.A2478P47 2007
811'.54--dc22

2007036818

Printed & bound by United Graphics. Inc.

First edition, 2008

Cover painting: Sarah McQuilkin
Book design: Rennie McQuilkin
Photo of author: Steven Jacob

Raymond Carver's "Late Fragment" (copyright © 1976, 1977,
1981, 1983, 1986, 1987, 1988 by Raymond Carver)
is used by permission of Grove/Atlantic, Inc.

Lines from "Elbows" copyright © 1997 by John Fox
are quoted by permission of John Fox
(The Institute for Poetic Medicine, www.poeticmedicine.org)

Antrim House
860.217.0023
AntrimHouse@comcast.net
www.AntrimHouseBooks.com
P.O. Box 111, Tariffville, CT 06081

ACKNOWLEDGEMENTS

Grateful acknowledgement is made to The Connecticut Hospice of Branford, CT, under whose auspices this book has been produced and to which all proceeds will be donated. Thanks also to the Hospice for permission to reprint certain poems that originally appeared in my earlier book, *Upon Their Quiet Altars,* also produced under the auspices of The Connecticut Hospice. I wish to thank John Fox for permission to quote from "Elbows," and Grove/Atlantic, Inc. for permission to quote Raymond Carver's "Late Fragment." In adition, I am grateful to Connecticut Community Care for selecting "Wall of Laughter" as a prize-winner in its recent poetry contest.

DEDICATIONS

As a poet and a volunteer, I have found myself writing poems based on situations that have taken place at The Connecticut Hospice in Branford, CT. This collection of poems is dedicated to the nurses, doctors, volunteers and workers at that Hospice and at all Hospice locations everywhere. What they contribute to the human experience is beyond measure. God bless them all.

This book is also dedicated to my loving partner in life, my wife Betty.

TABLE OF CONTENTS

TABLE OF CONTENTS

III. JOY

TABLE OF CONTENTS

IV. THE HUMAN FAMILY

INTRODUCTION

Since 1974 the Connecticut Hospice has cared for patients and their families as they cope with a terminal diagnosis. Since 1980 the Connecticut Hospice Arts Program, the first of its kind in the United States, has been integral in enhancing the lives of patients and family members. Artists, musicians, poets, therapists, and teachers facilitate creativity and emotional healing through the arts, both at our In-Patient Hospice Hospital and in Home Care across the state.

For hospice patients, their family members and the poets who visit and work with them, written and spoken words have the power to reach straight to the heart of one of life's most profound moments. Almost paradoxically, they also have the power to transcend and symbolize, as all art forms can, that which cannot be described in a straight-forward way. Sometimes the emotions are too difficult to voice without metaphor.

While those of us who work with hospice patients and families are called care-givers, countless times I have heard staff and volunteers say that they receive far more than they could ever give patients and family. This book is a testament to that truth. Bob Jacob joined the Arts Program as a volunteer who intended to read to patients and families, and perhaps help some patients and families write their own poetry. He planned both to speak and to listen, to honor and assist in giving voice to each individual spirit. He has certainly done all those things, and continues to do so, but what he did not predict was the impact that those interactions would have upon his own creative experience. Repeatedly after visiting our In-Patient units, he found himself moved to write about what had transpired, eventually building a collection of poems that he regards as a gift from the people who inspired them. As the poems grew in number, he magnanimously offered this bounty to The Connecticut Hospice for publication so that the proceeds could benefit our work. As he says in his poem "Wishes and Thanks," I say: *Thank you.*

Katherine Blossom Mascagna
Arts Director
The Connecticut Hospice

One thing I know: the only ones among you who will be truly happy are those who will have sought and found how to serve. —Albert Schweitzer, M.D.

I. HOSPICE

HOSPICE

Branford, Connecticut

Here, where a breeze speaks peace
    and shade cools concern,
boats like quiet ghosts slip by,
    memories bobbing with their bows.

From a large patio, grass slopes down
    to the ears of small waves,
hearing patients and their families
    mingle love with watchful waiting.

THE CONNECTICUT HOSPICE

When you walk
through the entrance
the world changes.

> Ego – gone.
> Artifice – gone.

Eyes speak of memories.
Hearts are shared.

> Over and over
> biblical words
> pulse in the air.

Love one another
love one another
love one another
love one another.

PEOPLE ASK

*When you are kind to people, and you pay
attention, you make a field of comfort around
them, and you get it back.*

— Anne Lamott

People ask, "How can you
read to the dying?"
My stock answer is,
"How can I not?"
This is my way to glide
past their own fear
of the inevitable.

Here is the real answer.

Many times when
I begin to read
their eyes are
anxious, frightened.
They know why they're here.

As I begin to read, or explain
what is about to be read,
they stare intently.
After one poem and into the second,

when the words begin
to touch and reach them,
their gaze begins to soften,
as though their life experience
and the words meet, become friends.
They are back in the world, and
sometimes, with those closest to death
a friendly smile arrives,
they ask for more,
trust the words
to carry them.

That is why I read at Hospice.

THE DIVINE

When a pastor is sitting in bed
with a hymnal in his lap
choosing music for his funeral

and when

he calmly tells you
that what is waiting for us
is the real living experience

and when

his loving wife hands you a copy
of one of his own poems
that will be part of his eulogy

and when

the pastor says, "You know, Bob,
the poems you just read to me
really aren't what you think they are:
they're music from the spheres"

it suddenly

is clear that being a volunteer
is really a gift from the divine.

VOLUNTEERS

move quietly among patients,
their presence deeply felt,
their work a cooling breeze
to those being devoured
by their own dying.

Volunteers, a ray of light
as they tremble
in the presence of God,
young and old
through song and words,
return and return
giving time and hearts
to souls seeking comfort.

If God is love,
they are the bearers of his promise.

IDT Meeting

Picture yourself surrounded
by people who care about you.
Some you know, some you don't.

Picture them discussing you,
your family, your pain,
drugs to help alleviate it.

Someone says you are declining
or you seem confused,
there is concern about your safety.

Someone says you're defying the prognosis,
maybe you can back off one drug,
add a new one to help you more.

There is discussion about a hospice benefit
or some way to help you with Medicare,
perhaps save you money on medications.

The people surrounding your needs
are nurses, social workers,
pharmacists, a doctor, chaplain, volunteer.

All of them meet once a week
without your knowledge, but
with nothing but your welfare in mind.

Picture some of them with
deep feelings for you, your family,
that go far beyond their jobs.

This is part of the miracle called *hospice*.

FORM

to serve
to serve
to serve

It's always there,
the form we fill out
for each patient visit.

Goals: (check which apply)
Relaxation, Relief of Symptons
(Loneliness/boredom), Relief of
Anxiety/Agitation, Enhancement
of Enviroment, Family Support

to help
to help
to help

Catherine lies quietly,
a former grade school teacher
with a beautiful smile,
dark brown eyes, soft voice.
She sighs after each poem,
then recites some back to me.

Reminiscences about her life,
her students, her love of poetry,
her recitations in class of
favorites Tennyson and Lowell.
It is a long, fruitful visit
where we share with each other.
I will check almost all
of the Goal boxes, plus one
that isn't listed, but should be:
"Gave me as much as she received."

Patient Family Responses:
Smiled/laughed, Engaged/
Focused on activity, Verbalized
enjoyment, Gratitude for visit,
Tearful, Shared life review,
Reminisced, Relaxed

>   to love
>   to love
>   to love

Joyce sits near her dying sister,
greets me with a sad smile.
She is an oncology nurse

and simply wants to talk
about their life as little girls,
how they jumped rope
and played hopscotch together.
In between a few poems
she is tearful, but direct
and filled with love.
Her heart beats in her eyes.
I will fill out the appropriate boxes
with my memory of her.

Suggested follow-up:
Ongoing arts support,
Ongoing assessment, Music,
Visual Arts, Literary arts

Copies of the form
will help other volunteers
and staff with insight

> to serve
> to help
> to love.

HOSPICE ROCKERS

How softly she holds the baby,
as if a dying child were a gift

to be returned,
which, of course, it is.

She is a "Rocker,"
as they are called,

because they sit for hours
in a large rocking chair

holding God's temporary gift.
Sometimes they croon

to the tiny infants.
Each in her own way

volunteers for this short journey.
I say angels rock them

gently with their wings
while they praise their beauty.

MEMORIAL SERVICE

The air is quiet
  when the roll call begins.
Sun drapes the lawn
  as loved ones carry
a flower, walking
  silently on grass
down the rows
  between folding chairs.
Not a whisper as
  each flower reverently
held is kissed and
  carefully, gently placed
in waiting baskets.
  Even the ripples
coming to shore
  fold in quietly.
Now an old woman
  barely able to walk
but determined, stops
  to gather breath,
then a small child
  sucking her bottle
holds her mother's hand.
  On and on they come

to honor loved ones.
  A distant bagpipe
weeps on a hill.
  Finally the baskets
are gathered as a boat
  pulls to dockside
then out again, full
  of memories and wishes,
everyone watching
  as they are spread
upon the water.
  Suddenly sun finds them
and they glisten brightly,
  the tide moving them
like receding angels.

PERSPECTIVE

Across from me in a diner
a man sits whining
about everyday problems.
I am tempted
to offer him a walk through
The Connecticut Hospice
on a day like many others:

This woman has breast cancer.
She is here to die.
Her husband and
their three teenage children
surround her like hovering angels.

In the next room
lies a forty-two-year-old man
with a plug in his throat.
Tears fill his eyes.
His wheezing breath, a dying flower.

In a public area five women,
three red-faced and weeping,
the other two stunned,

have just said goodbye to a father
who was always there for them.

Two rooms down
a lawyer with brain cancer,
father of two small children,
grasps for a memory,
his eyes a constant question mark.

Across the hall from him
a woman with shaved head,
large half moon scar across her skull,
sits mouthing silence, staring at air.

And in a room decorated for children
a mother beyond exhaustion
sits in a rocking chair
crooning to her tiny infant
as he quietly passes away.

I want to say to the man
seated in the diner,
Count your blessings,
even on a day when
aggravations cluster
and every breath is a wish.

GRACE

Tonight I sit watching
a Yankees-Red Sox game,
while in that hospital
whole lifetimes fade away.

Later I will kiss my wife
and sleep a sleep of soft dreams,
while in that hospital
the air will nod goodbye.

Tomorrow as the sun comes up
I will greet it with open arms,
while in that hospital
nurses will repeat their loving grace.

Nurses

We are each of us angels with only one wing.
And we can only fly embracing each other.

          — Luciano De Creschenzo

Nurses walk from room to room
with the voices of human angels,

their wings a white uniform,
their eyes a soft reflection

to souls wearing a dying cloak
of sheets, who gaze with unblinking eyes

into a heaven momentarily out of reach,
nurses bending to lift, support them,

offer them daily comfort.
Others glance in the nurses' direction,

proving they're still present,
reach out for a mercifcul word.

Each patient knows the brightness
of a nurse's angelic light

while crossing the void
to God's new world.

HOSPICE NURSE

There are things
said between people
that wrench the air,
like the hospice nurse
stopping me and saying
"You have captured exactly
what it is like here,"
and then as her arms
wrap me in a hug
she begins to weep,
an angel of mercy
in need of mercy.
I whisper to her
"You are the hero,
not me."

The Color Purple

She holds her wrinkled hands up
and asks what color I see.
I know why she asks.
"A beautiful rosy pink," I say.
She disagrees and says,
"I think they are dark, dark red."

She says in a quiet, dispassionate voice,
"When someone is dying
their fingertips change color."

Her hospital bed has been rolled
into a private area
facing large picture windows
overlooking Long Island Sound.
The water reflects a gray day.
She says, "Oh my! Look at that,
an angel flying across the water."
It's the bright white wake of a boat.

Almost immediately she spots
another angel above her.
Looking up I notice for the first time
etchings in the ceiling for patients

to see when their beds are rolled around:
an angel, balloons, Santa Claus, the moon.
Later when we roll her back to her room
I'll say, "Look, love, you're being mooned,"
which produces a soft laugh and smile.

Her head is almost skeletal,
which accentuates her
large, expressive eyes. The bones
of her upper chest and shoulders
protrude through dull white skin,
but her mind is clear, though slow.
She gives the impression
she is as light as the surrounding air.

Some of the poems I read
make her laugh, and when I ask her,
"If a man speaks in the forest
and there is no woman there to hear him,
is he still wrong?" she chuckles softly,
her cloudy blue eyes shining with mirth.

Some poems I read more than once.
The last stanza of the poem
"Let Evening Come" by Jane Kenyon,
I read over and over by request.

She says, "Please read it more slowly."

Let it come, as it will, and don't
be afraid. God does not leave us
comfortless, so let evening come.

During the fourth reading
she reaches out and holds my hand.
For the first time I notice
her finger nails are turning purple.

Freedom

In her early forties,
she is happy
to hear some poetry,
sighs after each poem, "Lovely."

Chatting, she says,
"My marriage of twenty years
ended in divorce.
My former husband relocated
to the mid-west, working at
a wonderful new job.
Yet, when I called with my
diagnosis, he immediately resigned,
came back to care for me and our son."

With a big smile
She says, "I'm happy
to be at Hospice,
to be free of pain
for the first time in months."

I HAVE LEARNED

that early morning air
fills my life with peace,
dew-drinking flowers with gratitude,
the chatter of birds with friendship.

These gifts of revelation come
from hospice patients
sharing thoughts,
positives, regrets, love given, received.

If you are feeling empty
and in need of a life refill,
volunteer, feel your soul revive.

II. Embroidering God's Voice

Upon Their Quiet Altars

From room to room
I find each bed a church

where family members gather
to offer love and prayer.

There are no granted wishes,
only tender mercies.

Poems spread like a holy grail
among the shining tears.

I have learned to read through
sorrow and aching hearts.

I have learned to place poetry
upon their quiet altars.

LIFE AT HOSPICE

It is a privilege
to look into the eyes
of the dying.
I see honesty,
a lack of guile,
a lack of walls.

They'll reach out,
hold my hand,
no strings attached,
just quiet consolation.

As I read to them
the force of the moment
locks them into memory,
and somehow the air
around me pulses
with life.

READING POETRY
TO HOSPICE PATIENTS

There is a small flower
called the Holy Spirit,
the quiet urge that roams deep,
embroidering God's voice
into the weight of our souls
that says listen and act,
and when you do, the warmth
of earth rises to meet you
while the veil of heaven lifts
as the spirit's thread
enters your voice, and creation
becomes a source of light.

Beautiful Words of Poetry

The dying speak volumes
with a glance or smile.

Beautiful words of poetry take them back,
then forward to where they are going.

The dying know this,
as they hold my hand like children.

Appreciation

Unshaven, skin mottled,
tubes in nose and throat,
yet, so gentle is this man's voice.
So well mannered in speech.
His words stroke my heart.

"It is really good of you to do
what you do. I so appreciate it.
I have written some poetry,
but nothing like the words
you're reading. What a blessing
to be read to like this."

He reaches out, holds my hand,
begins to tell me about
his life on Wall Street,
and New Rochelle,
the beautiful tree-lined streets,
his lifelong love of reading.
With no hint of fear in his voice
he comments about the mystery
of life, and life after death,
saying "No one really knows,

it's simply a matter of faith."
His soul seems open to the world.

It is humbling and a blessing
to share this time with him.
He has helped my soul expand,
to understand the needs of others,
and I thank him for it.
As I begin another poem
he weeps, says thank you again.

THE LANGUAGE OF DYING

He is rheumy-eyed, gesturing
like a symphony conductor,
but stops when asked if he
wants to hear some loving words.
He zeroes in on me
as I read first one
then another poem.
He motions for a halt,
his hands and voice addressing
the heavenly air
just over my right shoulder.
He is talking to
a deceased relative
in a language
beyond poetry, beyond
this world.

She is very old,
has lost all speech,
is startled by my presence.
I decide to read
a favorite, "Just For Today" —

Oh, God give me grace for this day,

*not for a lifetime, nor for next week, nor
for tomorrow, just for this day."*

As I continue, her eyes
look into mine
with relaxed interest
then, not quite a smile,
almost like a mother
recognizing a son
speaking his love for her.

CRADLED LOVE

A poem I read to patients
is called "Elbows."
I introduce it by saying
"Who would write a poem about elbows?"
They laugh and nod in agreement, but
then I say, "Wait until you hear
what this wonderful poet, John Fox,
does in the last part of this poem."

> *The deepest current of love*
> *is not found in the heart.*
> *That is the certain spring,*
> *the natural ease, the flow*
> *from the mountaintop.*
> *The greatest current of love*
> *rushes forward in the choice*
> *to make a cradle of the body.*

Recently as I read these lines,
the eyes of a cancer patient widened
and she exclaimed to her husband,
"My God, John, it's another sign."
She explained that in a recent dream
she saw Jesus, his eyes filled with love,
his arms not spread wide,
but each one bent at the elbow
forming a cradle for her.

WISHES AND THANKS

To the man
  whose hand I held
    as he held his wife's
      and wept, who said
        "Thank you for
          the loving words,
            I wish you peace."

To the woman
  curled toward me
    who whispered I was
      a bouquet of words,
        and kept asking
          for more poems,
            I wish you heaven.

And to the man with
  troubled breathing
    who nodded his
      desire for poetry,
        and who slowly rasped
          a poem from memory,
            I say, *Thank you.*

CROSSING THE BAR AT HOSPICE

An old man holds his wife's hand
who looks bemused in her bed
at my offer of loving words.
He accepts on her behalf.
After I read the first poem
he says, "My favorite is 'Crossing The Bar'"
which he begins to recite from memory.

   Sunset and evening star,
   And one clear call for me!
   And may there be no moaning of the bar,
   When I put out to sea,

   But such a tide as moving seems asleep,
   Too full for sound of foam,
   When that which drew from out the boundless deep
   Turns home again.

   Twilight and evening bell,
   And after that the dark!
   And may there be no sadness of farewell,
   When I embark;

   For tho' from out our bourne of Time and Place

The flood may bear me far,
I hope to see my pilot face to face
When I have crossed the bar.

He says, "Don't know if I got it all.
I used to be a ham actor
and my mind has been fried to a crisp."

I hand him a copy of this poem
by Alfred Lord Tennyson,
which was given to me for the first time
just five minutes earlier
as a poem I might read to patients,
and yes, he had it word for word.

THE WRECK OF THE HESPERUS

Lying there it's as though
she is climbing back into herself,
so concave and curled,
head pushed into her chest,
eyes tightly closed,
yet I sense a need,
so loving words are offered
and accepted in a whisper.

After two short poems
her eyes look up at me
as she barely mumbles
"I know a poem by heart."

Now on my knees
next to her down-turned head,
I ask for a recitation.
She moves her bone thin arms
like a child about to recite,
as she forms the title and author
in memorized respect:

"The Wreck of the Hesperus"
by Henry Wadsworth Longfellow

It was the schooner Hesperus,
That sailed the wintery sea...
And the skipper had taken his little daughter...
To bear him company...

She gathers her breath to continue
In a slow interrupted cadence.

Blue were her eyes as the fairy flax...
Her cheeks like the dawn of day...
And her bosom white as the hawthorn bud,
That ope in the month of May...

She stops. "Sorry, I always get stuck here,
because it reminds me of my father...
who I loved very much..."

Her voice is barely audible,
trying to put words together:

The skipper he stood beside the helm,
His pipe was in his mouth...
And he watched how the veering flaw did blow...
The smoke now West, now South.

Silence. Another apology.

I tell her that human desire
is a miraculous thing,
and it is a miracle she has remembered
three stanzas of a twenty-two stanza poem.

She is dying, though her spirit
produces a faint smile.
I am thankful for it.

THE READING

She is very old, sitting slightly tilted
to one side in a wheelchair.
I drop to one knee
to be on eye level with her,
and ask if she would like to hear
some loving words of poetry.
Smiling, she says, "Yes Father,"
mistaking me for a priest,
and I wonder if the
dark slacks and deep blue shirt
were such a good idea today.
After reading the poem
"Just For Today" by Marjorie Holmes,
I ask if she would like
a copy to read.
Misinterpreting the word "read,"
she begins to read it back to me,
apologizing for her lack of glasses,
but pronouncing each word with
deep emotion, in a quiet quavering voice.
All the surrounding hospital noise
slowly fades into the background
as we enter a private cocoon of poetry,
and it occurs to me that
were I on both knees it would
be more than appropriate.

Forgive Yourself

Earth teach me humility
  as blossoms are humble with beginning.

We are sitting in a small
  common area overlooking
a cove of calm water.
  She is a black woman,
forty-three years old
  with deep brown eyes
and a warm, inviting gaze.

Earth teach me stillness
  as the grasses are stilled by light.

With deep religious feeling
  she quotes from the
New Testament in a
  lilting Jamaican voice
that sings with premature age.

Earth teach me limitation
  as an ant which crawls on the ground.

She is polite, frightened and tense,
  but mostly she has regrets,
saying over and over
  "I have so many regrets."

I tell her life is an experiment that
    sometimes fails, and
we all disappoint others and ourselves.

Earth teach me caring
    as the mother who secures her young.

I read line after line as
    we gift one another with words,
her regrets not like self pity,
    but anger aimed at herself.
She wants to discuss religion
    and her belief that we can
only be saved through Jesus Christ.
    I talk of the Old Testament,
the Koran, Buddhism, God's grace to all.

Earth teach me courage
    as the tree which stands alone.

I am her only visitor
    as she sits in her wheelchair
so I tell a joke and she laughs,
    then grasps my hand, looks out
the window at the water
    while tears run down her cheeks,
and says again, over and over,
    "but I have so many regrets."

(*Italicized sections comprise a Ute Prayer.*)

LOVING WORDS

for Domonique

I was hoping she would
still be here, and she is.
Our last visit she spoke of regrets
and I wanted to reach out again,
hoping to cancel more of them.
Approaching her bed
I said, "Do you remember me?"
She said, "Loving word man,
my loving word man."
She was relaxed and smiling;
her eyes never left mine while
she reached for my hand, saying
"You have graced my life –
I will never forget you."

Some words are spoken
like arrows to the heart.
These rushed like a river to mine.
"Here is a gift for you," she added,
handing me a large laminated
copy of *The Lord's Prayer*
surrounded by a multi-colored

stained glass window.
Made by volunteers
for a patient to give as a gift
to a loving family member.
She said, "Will you promise
to keep this near you?"
I replied, "Not only it, but you."

AS I READ TO YOU

your mouth
forms silent words,

as if dancing
in a lover's embrace.

Your head turns
toward my loving words.

Your eyes fill with clouds
moving you to heaven.

THE PRESENT

Every poet at some time
    should be a birthday present.

He should be presented
    to a Hospice patient

by family members gathered
    around the patient's bed

on her 89th birthday as
    a part of her celebration.

Family will say, "Here is a special
    present for you, Aunt Clara."

The poet, as he reads loving words,
    will notice the patient's

extra bright smile, her dark
    brown eyes lit like candles.

III. Joy

Young Woman with Soft Blue Eyes

Your gentle smile radiates
with loving concentration,
an expression of satisfaction
shining under your baldness,
when suddenly you ask,
"Do you hear my dogs barking?"
and I say, "What are their names?"
You reply, "Molly and Mickey.
They were mine when I was little.
Can you hear them barking?"

Then I begin to read the poem
"Let Evening Come" by Jane Kenyon.
When I get to the last stanza —

Let it come as it will, and don't
be afraid. God does not leave us
comfortless, so let evening come" —

you smile and nod,
looking off into the distance
at your pets waiting to greet you.

CONFESSION

She is very elderly,
but still sharp and aware.
In between readings
our conversation roams
over marriage, the Great Depression,
families, hers from Austria,
mine from Ireland and England.
She says, "We're all immigrants."
Years ago she was impressed by
President Roosevelt when he spoke
to the D.A.R. and started
by saying, "Fellow immigrants."

Then I read "In The Year of My Birth,"
one of my poems in which
milk is forty-three cents a gallon,
bread seven cents a loaf.
I tell her I love to read this poem
to young people because their jaws
drop when gas is just ten cents a gallon.
She asks my year of birth.
When I say 1932 she smiles,
says she was born in 1929.
As I read another poem
her expression turns serious.
After I finish she says,
"I lied. I was born in 1921."
Our laughter fills the room.

CONFESSON II

Her eyes are full of tension
as I offer loving words.
She accepts, replies,
"As long as it isn't Godly Pablum."
Laying aside a Godly poem
and pulling up a chair,
I hand her a copy of
"Late Fragments" by Raymond Carver,
the poem asking *Did you get*
what you wanted from life even so?
and the poet answers, *I did,*
indicating to be beloved on earth
was his greatest earthly desire.
She hands it back with the words,
"This doesn't apply to me."
For the first time her loneliness
lies heavy between us,
so I ask if she would like to hear a poem of mine
with a line that was a gift,
and she comments that the gift of words
has happened to her too,
a hint of possible poetic connection.

I explain that I love Autumn.
I read my seven-line poem "Late Autumn,"
its last line totally unexpected –
"Let us hail one another as a kind hearted gift" –

which wrinkles her brow,
and while her hands flutter
her bone thin arm reaches
almost rudely past me
to the drawer of a bedside table,
where a small piece of handwritten
paper has been hidden.
She grabs it, whisks it between us,
reads a three-line haiku
about four dying women in a room
watching sailboats glide past their windows.
She immediately puts it back,
slams the drawer shut, asks for an opinion,
while I congratulate her on getting
the exact count of syllables correct
and say it is a beautiful poem
which I'd like to see again, but am denied.

Now, to my amazement
she tells me she is a Franciscan,
explaining she is in the third order
where she may marry,
although she never had the opportunity.
Suddenly her nervous edginess
expands as a nurse drops a tray.
"That won't do, that won't do," she says.

All the while we've been talking
I've had the feeling something is missing,
until finally she looks into my eyes,
and without a hint of hesitation says,
"I have a secret to tell you.
My life has been so lonely
I once thought of ending it, but
because of my Christian belief
didn't go through with it."

I take her hand in mine.
We sit holding each other's thoughts.

VOLUNTEER

I knelt on one knee
   to be on eye level with her
sitting in a wheelchair
   and read some loving words,
and after reading, on impulse
   asked, still on one knee,
"Will you marry me?"
Her old frail body
   shook with delighted laughter.

You Have to Understand

You with the finger pointing,
angels in your lake-blue eyes,
voice like a song,
you have to stop saying,

"See her, she needs your poems too.
She's a lonely, lovely lady,
and that old woman near the door
she needs loving words as well."

You have to understand.
God is calling you too.
Your time for receiving has arrived.

Soon

The first thing I notice about him
is his snowy white hair,
the shine and wave of it.

His two friends laughingly say
the nurses and volunteers
constantly comb it to make waves.

He and his friends laugh
as I read a funny poem.
They seem to rejoice in their friendship.

Suddenly he says, "My wife died
nine years ago tomorrow,"
and then as if in a revelation,

"The dying know
when they are about to go.
The night she died

we were watching T.V.
when I noticed her staring at me.
I said, 'Why aren't you watching T.V.'?

and she said softly
'I want to look at you.'
Later when I came back from the bathroom

she was gone, just like that.
I immediately called our minister
and the funeral home.

Why did I rush to do that?
I'll never forgive myself.
Why didn't I hold her one last time?"

Soon he'll be able to hold her forever.

Joy

Beautiful pale blue eyes
shine with mirth.
Even as muscles fail her
in these last days of life,
she asks to hear something funny.

"If a man speaks in the forest, and
there's no woman around to hear him,
is he still wrong?"

She loves it, tells a joke
about a woman who gives
instructions to be cremated,
her ashes spread over water
so they sink to the ocean floor,
where fish eat them, then
when they're caught she
is part of a gourmet meal.

I smile at her remarkable spirit.
As I begin a humorous poem
her bedside phone rings.
She can't lift so
I prop it against her shoulder.

A friend from California
who has learned of her situation
is calling, begins to weep.

"Don't cry. My lawyer cried too.
People shouldn't be crying.
Here, I want you to picture
a big, beautiful sunflower
shining in bright sunlight.
It lasts a long time.
Then the sky turns gray.
The sunflower wilts,
dies, as we all do.
That's life, love. That's life."

Consoling a friend
this remarkable survivor
of the Holocaust smiles at me.
The love in her eyes
radiates like angels who
sometimes visit these rooms.

Her name was Joy.

THE PACT

She is an eighty-five-year-old
former high school teacher
with lively eyes and conversation.

She likes the silver in my hair.
I compliment her on her own
whose brilliant white frames her peace.

She has a long lined pad next to her
with a list of things to accomplish.
Each time she crosses one off another is added.

She has been battling cancer for three years,
talks about her deep faith in God
and casually mentions her pact with him.

Her words spoken so quietly
but with deep, deep conviction
grow in my mind like tiny flowers.

"I told God I would accept cancer
if he would promise to cure one child
for every year I manage to survive."

The determination in her words and eyes
says maybe one more will be saved.

CONNECTIONS

A patient says, "Something wonderful
happened to me yesterday.
Family were around my bed
when someone asked
my twelve-year-old grandson
who he wanted to be like when he's older.
He put his hand on my shoulder
and said, 'I want to be just like him.'"
I comment, "You must be very happy."
He smiles, reaches out, holds my hand.
For a moment the love of caring
is shared between us,
fills us to the brim.

The face of a man the next bed over
is framed in a smile
as I read poetry to him,
yet when he speaks
the words slide out as gibberish,
but with serious intent.

Across the room a black man
in a wheelchair, eyes closed,
head in hand, rolls back and forth.
I ask if he is all right.

"Yes, I'm meditating about life."
On the wall near his bed, drawings
of two children and grandchildren.
His words are filled with
the light of experience.
"I was a fool. Always after the ladies,
so many I've lost count,
lost some loves, but moved on."
I ask how many children he has.
"Four children, seventeen grandchildren."

Just then the man who speaks nonsense
tries to climb out of bed.
While I go to his side
to keep him from falling,
the commotion brings a nurse.
The man shouts "Sons-o'-bitches!"
but finally lies down, the air
purple with his mumbled curses.

The black man chuckles, and says,
"I try to watch out for him.
He's more screwed up than me,
can't tell which way is up.
You know we have an obligation
to care for one another."

Taking Flight

You are small, shrunken,
lying on your side

like a dying bird
on white sheets,

your hands claw-like
drawn under your chin,

head tilted toward me
listening to poetry.

The small of your mouth
is like a silent surprise.

I lean close
to speak loving lines

as your cloudy gray eyes
slowly close forever.

WAITING

A small Puerto Rican lady
in a bright red robe
with dice pictured on it
almost reluctantly says yes
to the offer of loving words.
As I read some poems
her eyes travel from me
to deep inside herself,
hiding her glance
as I tell her I have twelve
grandchildren and ask
if she has any, and
she answers twenty-seven
which fills me with awe
since she is only sixty,
but I continue and then
ask if she would like
to hear a love poem
written for my wife
of fifty-five years,
after which she wants
to know if my love
is still very strong

and when I say yes
she beats her fist
against her heart saying,
"Love is everything,
it is everything"
as she stares at the door
where visitors arrive,
but none appear.

SPECIAL LADY

At 89 her gray hair is lovely,
"naturally wavy," she says.
Her eyes a bit flirtatious.
She is erect in a chair
next to her bed on which
a teenage great grandson sits,
his mother close by.

Her name is Mary and she
seems at ease with death,
saying she is looking forward
to seeing old friends, family
who have gone before her.
She says, "I hope I get a good seat,"
implying heaven is a theatre
with preferred seating for those
waiting to greet newcomers.
I share my mother's last hours,
how she brought me close
and said, "Everybody says hello."

Mary says, "My sons are wimps,
all they do is cry when they visit."
Then she smiles, pats her hair,
asks if I *really* like it.
As I tell her yes I also say
her sons aren't wimps,
but showing their love for her.

Her granddaughter relates
how she took her to a hairdresser
and afterwards Mary insisted
they go to choose a casket for her.
The granddaughter was appalled,
but did it, and then helped
her choose the music
and readings for her funeral.

After reading five serious poems
I ask if she would like to hear
something in a lighter vein.
She answers in the affirmative
so I read: *If a man speaks in the
forest and there's no woman around
to hear him, is he still wrong?*
Both she and her granddaughter
answer with an emphatic "Yes!"

Then the granddaughter asks Mary,
"Should I tell him about the
plaque hanging in your house?"
Mary chuckles, winks at me, says yes.
It reads, *If they can land one man
on the moon, why can't they
all go there?*

SAFE PLACE

So soft her gaze,
her look searching.

One minute listening,
the next staring upward.

Her body angling away,
then turning back

to murmur "Thank you,
please read another poem."

In her fifties she
seems almost detached

from her present situation.
I read "Late Fragments"

by Raymond Carver,
a beautiful short poem

about being beloved on earth.
She points at the ceiling.

I ask why. She replies,
"That's my safe place."

"Your safe place?"
"Yes."

"Why is it safe?"
"Your words appear there."

Then, staring upward she repeats
the words that I have offered.

HUMOR

Behind thick glasses
there shines a biting
sense of humor.

She never married.
I tell her I have been
happily married 55 years.

"You're full of baloney!"

After I stop laughing
we talk of favorite drinks,
hers, martini, mine, white wine.

"So, you're a sissy boy!"

When I stop laughing again
we reminisce about WW II and
her favorites, the Andrew Sisters.

She sings completely off key,
*Mairsey doats and doazy doats
and little amesy divey, a kiddlley*

divey too wouldn't you.
I congratulate her on
her lovely singing voice.

It's her turn to laugh.

HOLY LAUGHTER

She is elderly and emaciated,
yet I see joy and humor
in her pale blue eyes.
After I read some grandchild poems
she relates with pride
how a grandson recently passed
his driving test on the first try.
She laughs as some jokes are shared.
Suddenly she says,

> "It took a long time
> for cancer to catch up with me.
> Sixteen years of on and off
> chemo and radiation treatments.
> I had a wonderful doctor,
> always had a joke to tell.
> He'd say, 'Oh no, not you again.'
> I loved the man.
> He died four years ago.
> Do you think we'll meet in heaven?"

In a situation like this
my answer is simple.
I say, "He's waiting patiently for you.
He has a joke he's dying to tell you."

She laughs out loud.

IV. The Human Family

READING POETRY

This is how it is —
reading, sadness seeps in.

As families sing a song of grief
we breathe in harmony.

For a few moments our eyes meet,
and we share the human family.

Love flows from the dying
as boundaries disappear,

and we cradle one another
with our tender needs.

Beyond Words

The patient is sunken
into his pillow, his hands
deeply veined, cheeks mottled red.
Breathing tubes hang from his nose,
but his eyes still shine with life.
Family hover around the bed,
hold his hands, murmur quietly to him.
I approach and say, "I am a volunteer
who reads loving words to patients.
Would you like to hear some?"
From deep within the pillow he says,
"I am surrounded by them."

BLESSED SCENE

The father is propped up
  on his death bed,
mouth slightly agape,
  eyes staring at air.
He wears earphones
  that play calming music,
while a daughter in the glow
  of morning caresses him
and a son bent forward
  in prayer holds his hand.
I, unnoticed, back away
  from a scene so sacred
the Trinity comes to mind.

WALL OF LAUGHTER

for Helen

Four adult daughters
surround her bed,
all of whom say yes
to a reading of loving words.
She continues to turn the pages
of *Vogue* magazine,
making humorous comments.

"Look at them, they all look
like they need a good meal.
If my hair looked like that
they'd lock me up."

Her daughters chuckle and giggle
until the title of the poem
"Elbows" is announced.
As I begin to read, Helen begins
a lament on how ugly
her elbows are and have been forever.

"Oh Mom don't be ridiculous."
"Momma you don't have ugly elbows."

"That's absolutely stupid."
" I never heard anything so crazy."

As I stop reading, her daughters
begin to laugh. She holds up
her elbows for all of us to see.

"See how pointy they are?
Once I went to a cocktail party,
spent a fortune on a dress,
and my elbows ruined the whole effect."

The laughter is so loud now
it sounds like a party.
I've given up on the poem,
and am starting to worry
about staff coming
to question my presentation.
When her eyes lock on mine
she has a wry grin.
I suddenly realize
she has begun to protect them
from what lies ahead
with a wall, a wall of laughter.

AT BEDSIDE

The movement
was so quiet and slow
it took me by surprise.

She was exhausted,
her mouth a shrunken O,
barely breathing,
and when I read the
first two lines of a poem —
  And did you get what
  you wanted from life even so? —
I did not expect

her small fragile hand
to slowly lift and point
at her husband
bowed in prayer.

FORGIVENESS

The weak can never forgive.
Forgiveness is an attribute of the strong."

— Mahatma Gandhi

After I read a third poem
he reaches out, holds my hand
and begins to speak
in a low halting voice.

"I was really a stupid jerk
in my early forties.
Heavy drinker. Cheated on my wife
so she divorced me."

The air between us is still,
I know I should just listen.

"I have two daughters
who wouldn't talk to me.
I didn't care. Self absorbed.
So much crap going on
in the family I didn't
even attend one daughter's wedding.
Did go to the second girl's, but
can you imagine not going to the other?"

He has tears on both cheeks.
His grasp is very strong.

"Two days ago the daughter
whose wedding I missed came,
and I asked her for forgiveness.
We both began to cry and
she said she forgave me."

He has given his daughter
The best gift she will ever receive.
I tell him so.

PRISONER

When the guards quietly
stepped outside the room,

and the nurses helped you
hold your mother,

did the leg and arm shackles
weigh more than your heart,

and did your sobbing promises
to stop all drugs flower in her eyes?

Your thoughtful after-visit thank you note
speaks of a changed life, a straight path.

May our prayers for your mother
dwell in you as well.

More Than You Know

The eyes and smile
of this thin and frail
elderly woman
are soft, welcoming.
She loves poetry,
reacts with happiness
as I read each poem.
A grandchild poem melts her.

"My daughter adopted
twin Romanian babies,
Tina and Marie.
They're seven years old now.
Doing very well in first grade."

Her gestures become eloquent,
almost those of a ballerina,
as she relives moments
with her precious granddaughters.

"Tina is more child-like.
Plays with dolls,
feeds, dresses, talks to them.
She will make a good mother.
Marie is serious.

Once she asked me why
her mother threw her away.
I explained that she
couldn't feed or clothe them
so she put them in an
orphanage where they
would be well fed and safe.
She likes to cuddle on my lap
while I read stories to her."

Her eyes brim at this.
She looks away.
I read a short poem
as she collects herself,
talk about my own grandchildren,
the spread of their ages,
how each is an individual.

She leans forward,
asks me to retrieve
a manila envelope
from a bedside table
that's full of greeting cards.

"Please open the green envelope

with 'Granny' written on it.
Marie gave it to me.
Read what it says."

The cover of the card has
a mommy chicken with a chick.
Inside, in rough child's printing
that starts at the top
and runs down one side —

I

  LOV

    YOU

        MOOR

       THAN

      YOU

        THINK

          I DO

GATHERING TREASURE

In a corner of the room
an elderly woman
propped against pillows.

A granddaughter holds her
skeletal spotted hand,
applying red nail polish.

Near the granddaughter,
her husband, his hand
supporting their new daughter,
helping her sit on the fluffy covers,

a small seven-month angel
in overalls and frilly shirt,
with lively blue eyes
and pacifier in her mouth,
small hands stirring the air.

Loving words are read –

> *May God be in my heart and my loving.*
> *May God be in my mind and my thinking.*
> *May God be in my ears and my listening.*
> *May God be in my eyes and my seeing.*

At one end of the bed,
Madison, a great granddaughter.
At the other end Jean, a great grandmother
preparing to take this moment with her.

Passing Along

His two-year-old chin
rests on his mother's shoulder.
Inquisitive blue eyes stare at me
under hair soft as silk.
He smiles. I melt.
      He is visiting
his great-grandmother
who sits propped up in bed,
her gaze slightly vague,
yet she wants to hear
some loving words of poetry.
She says softly, "You have to receive
as well as give love."
      Her bed is surrounded by
a sister, daughter, two granddaughters,
and little Max, who is very content.
His mother says all of them
live together with several dogs,
so he has love all around him.
As does his great-grandmother
at this ending time of life.
      As I read, there is a feeling
of being in a bubble of acceptance,
where a passing along is taking place.
I can imagine Max, years from now
being reminded of the time
great-grandmother Ruth
held and kissed him one more time.

STILL HERE

Teenage boy in white shirt
silently sitting next to
unconscious grandmother,
his face down on her bed,
both arms outstretched,
one hand on her foot.

Three Ladies

One, very old, tilts
like a tired lily
against soft pillows,
her head caressed
by a gray-haired daughter
murmuring assurance.

Each time the elder starts,
as if saying *No
I will not die yet,*
her eyes open
to see a granddaughter
holding her hand,
watching, learning.

WHEN IT'S TIME

Will you sing a song
    while dying
and will you sing it
    at the top of your voice
and will a daughter
    sing along with you
and will your wife of 67 years
    hum along in quiet harmony
and will the song be
    "Watching All The Girls Go By"
from a musical called
    The Most Happy Fella?

THE WHOLE BALL OF WAX

In "Late Fragment"
Raymond Carver wrote:

*And did you get what
you wanted from this life, even so?
I did.
And what did you want?
To call myself beloved, to feel myself
beloved on the earth.*

I have lost count
of the times I have read
this to hospice patients,
standing at bedside
reading slowly, deliberately.

Today a man propped up,
surrounded by family,
looked at me and said,
"That's the whole ball of wax,
isn't it, everything else is crap."

I agreed, his family nodded,
and then I took his words
home with me where
I always worry about crap.

When am I going to learn?

Conversion

She sits very straight with
eyes staring, a blank expression.

After offering some loving words
I am being scrutinized, evaluated.

Then in clipped, precise tones she says,
"All right, you may read something."

I choose a poem with Godly blessings.
In her almost curt manner —

"Do you know this quotation:
'God is and you seek to speak' "?

While pondering this I note
no rings, a Godly quote,

and think perhaps a religious.
In stark, stiff words —

"My husband died. I am a widow
with two children, four grandchildren."

With permission I read my poem
"Just So You'll Know"

which carries a message about
a grandparent greeting a grandchild

in the beauty of eternity.
With tears in her eyes

she beckons me forward,
plants a kiss on my cheek.

The afternoon begins to glow.

Just So You'll Know

for Emma Regina Bour

When I was a small boy
my parents would walk me
over warm cement sidewalks
in Queens, New York City,
to a place called Forest Park,
a refuge of sorts, away from
train and traffic noise,
to a special boating pond
where children would sail
toy boats of all sizes.
Some boats tied to a string
were walked around pond's edge,
but I always pushed my boat outward
to catch a breeze across the sea.

Yesterday at seven weeks old,
you lay cradled in the crook of
my left arm, where I cradled
that small boat.
Your entire body fit along
my forearm, with your
bootied feet cupped in my hand.

Like a sail catching wind
your arms and hands fluttered,
and I gazed closely at your perfect
infant features, at your fingers
the length of my thumb's width.

Like my sailboat, when
I finally release you
to begin your own voyage,
and when the breeze
of your breath ceases,
I will be there to gather you in.

Bob Jacob was born in Brooklyn, NY. He played stickball on the city's streets and baseball for the Ozone Park Braves in Queens, NY. He inherits his love of poetry from his father, who wrote verse about family love. Bob served in the army during the Korean War and has been against war ever since. Upon discharge, he worked as a traveling salesman for a filing supply company in New England. In the sixties he became a partner in an office & computer supply company in Hartford. In the mid-eighties he and his wife, Betty, bought and operated Brook Farm Inn in Lenox, Massachusetts. They housed poets free of charge and ran a poetry series at Herman Melville's home in Pittsfield, bringing in some of the great poets of our time for readings and conversation. In the mid-nineties Bob and his wife moved back to Connecticut, where he created VERSEtility BOOKS, selling signed poetry editions with almost all the profits going directly to the poets. This business was active for ten years, during which over $100,000 was sent to the poets. The correspondence for VERSEtility BOOKS is now housed in the Beineke Library at Yale University. Also during the 1990's Bob began to read poetry to cancer support groups in central Connecticut. In addition, he made his large collection of poems available to churches, chaplains, and individual cancer and MS patients. For seven years he has been reading poetry as a hospice volunteer at The Connecticut Hospice Hospital in Branford. He has also been a hospice volunteer at the Visiting Nurse Association in East Hartford, and is at present a hospice volunteer through the VNA at St. Francis Hospital in Hartford, reading to home-bound patients. "Upon Their Quiet Altars," a short selection of his hospice poems, was published in 2004. Bob says his hospice work is the most fulfilling thing he has ever done, aside from being married for fifty-five years to the girl of his dreams and raising three children who have produced twelve grandchildren.

COLOPHON

This book has been set in Perpetua, designer Eric Gill's most
celebrated typeface. The clean, chiseled look of the
font reflects its creator's stonecutting work.

For discussion topics and writing suggestions, as well as
additional biography, images and poems, visit the Antrim
House website: www.AntrimHouseBooks.com/seminar.

To order Antrim House titles
contact the publisher at

Antrim House
P.O. Box 111
Tariffville, CT 06081
860-217-0023
www.AntrimHouseBooks.com
AntrimHouse@comcast.net